Baby Animals in the Wild!

Gorilla Infants in the Wild

by Marie Brandle

Bullfrog Books

Ideas for Parents and Teachers

Bullfrog Books let children practice reading informational text at the earliest reading levels. Repetition, familiar words, and photo labels support early readers.

Before Reading
- Discuss the cover photo. What does it tell them?

- Look at the picture glossary together. Read and discuss the words.

Read the Book
- "Walk" through the book and look at the photos. Let the child ask questions. Point out the photo labels.

- Read the book to the child, or have him or her read independently.

After Reading
- Prompt the child to think more. Ask: Gorilla moms groom their infants. Can you name any other animals that do this?

Bullfrog Books are published by Jump!
5357 Penn Avenue South
Minneapolis, MN 55419
www.jumplibrary.com

Library of Congress Cataloging-in-Publication Data

Names: Brandle, Marie, 1989– author.
Title: Gorilla infants in the wild / by Marie Brandle.
Description: Minneapolis, MN: Jump!, Inc., [2023]
Series: Baby animals in the wild!
Includes index. | Audience: Ages 5–8
Identifiers: LCCN 2022009737 (print)
LCCN 2022009738 (ebook)
ISBN 9798885240680 (hardcover)
ISBN 9798885240697 (paperback)
ISBN 9798885240703 (ebook)
Subjects: LCSH: Gorilla—Infancy—Juvenile literature.
Classification: LCC QL737.P94 B725 2023 (print)
LCC QL737.P94 (ebook)
DDC 599.88413/92—dc23/eng/20220315
LC record available at https://lccn.loc.gov/2022009737
LC ebook record available at https://lccn.loc.gov/2022009738

Editor: Eliza Leahy
Designer: Molly Ballanger

Photo Credits: uzuri/Shutterstock, cover; Jrleyland/iStock, 1; This N That/Shutterstock, 3; Nick Fox/Shutterstock, 4, 23tr; Igorcorinne/Dreamstime, 5; Ben Birchall - PA Images/Getty, 6–7; ZSSD/Minden Pictures/SuperStock, 8; Suzi Eszterhas/Minden Pictures/SuperStock, 9, 20–21, 23tl; TiggyMorse/iStock, 10–11; Saaaaa/Dreamstime, 12–13, 23bl; Martin Lindsay/Alamy, 14–15; Brina L. Bunt/Shutterstock, 16; Eric Baccega/age fotostock/SuperStock, 17; Minden Pictures/SuperStock, 18–19, 23br; Teresa Considine/Shutterstock, 22; Eric Gevaert/Dreamstime, 24.

Printed in the United States of America at Corporate Graphics in North Mankato, Minnesota.

Table of Contents

Grow and Play

A gorilla infant is a baby.

It stays with Mom.
Mom holds it.

The infant drinks Mom's milk.

It grows!

The infant has dark hair.
Its hair grows, too.

hair

Mom grooms it.
She picks bugs out.

The infant rides
on Mom's back.

It holds on with its
hands and feet.

It walks on its own!

It explores the rain forest.

leaf

The infant and
Mom find food.

They eat leaves.

The infant plays.
It climbs.

It swings!

It lives in a troop.

troop

It plays with other gorilla infants.

They grow up together.

Parts of a Gorilla Infant

What are the parts of a gorilla infant? Take a look!

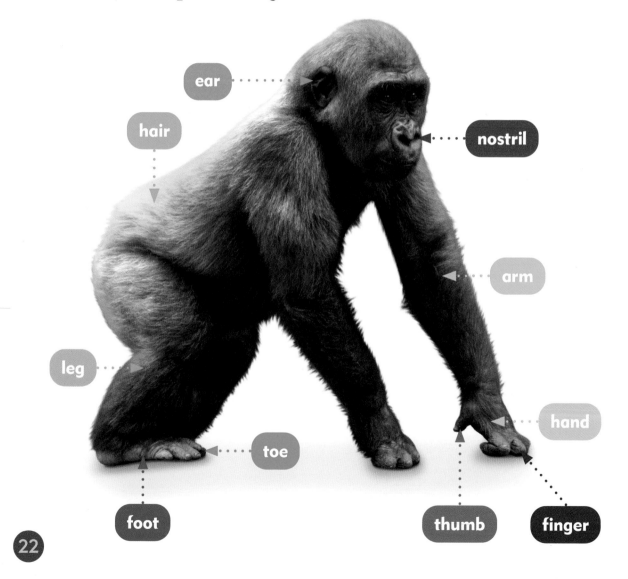

ear

hair

nostril

arm

leg

hand

toe

foot

thumb

finger

Picture Glossary

grooms
Cleans.

infant
A young gorilla.

rain forest
A thick, tropical forest where a lot of rain falls.

troop
A group of gorillas.

Index

To Learn More

Finding more information is as easy as 1, 2, 3.

❶ Go to www.factsurfer.com

❷ Enter "gorillainfants" into the search box.

❸ Choose your book to see a list of websites.